THE
TRANSFORMATIONAL
POWER
OF
EXECUTIVE TEAM
ALIGNMENT

THE
TRANSFORMATIONAL
POWER
OF
EXECUTIVE TEAM
ALIGNMENT

ORGANIZATIONAL SUCCESS BEYOND
YOUR WILDEST DREAMS

MILES KIERSON

Published by Advantage, Charleston, South Carolina.
Member of Advantage Media Group.

ADVANTAGE is a registered trademark and the Advantage colophon is a trademark of Advantage Media Group, Inc.

Printed in the United States of America

ISBN: 978-1-59932-105-9
Library of Congress Control Number: 2006940051

Most Advantage Media Group titles are available at special quantity discounts for bulk purchases for sales promotions, premiums, fundraising, and educational use. Special versions or book excerpts can also be created to fit specific needs.

For more information, please write: Special Markets, Advantage Media Group, P.O. Box 272, Charleston, SC 29402 or call 1.866.775.1696.

TABLE OF CONTENTS

INTRODUCTION: **WHY YOU SHOULD READ THIS BOOK** | 7

CHAPTER ONE: **THE TRUTH ABOUT CURRENT EXECUTIVE TEAMS** | 15
    A Typical Executive Team | 17
    A Typical Executive | 20
    A Typical CEO, President, or Other Senior Executive | 24

CHAPTER TWO: **DEFINING ALIGNMENT** | 29
    Ownership | 35
    Alignment and Commitment | 36
    Alignment is An Individual Capability | 39
    Executive Team Alignment | 40
    The Top 10 Benefits of Executive Team Alignment | 45

CHAPTER THREE **KEY ELEMENTS OF A SUCCESSFULLY ALIGNED TEAM** | 51
    A Shared Understanding of Alignment | 53
    An Understanding of the Decision-Making Process | 56
    Saying What Needs to Be Said | 64
    Being Committed to Each Other's Success | 68

CHAPTER FOUR: **SUSTAINING ALIGNMENT** | 75
    For the CEO | 80
    For the Team Member | 86

CHAPTER FIVE: **GETTING INTO ACTION NOW** | 89
    What to Do Until the Doctor Comes (So to Speak) | 90
    So What Do You do? | 94
    What to Do in Dealing with Others | 102
    This is a Journey | 105

CONCLUSION: **ALIGNING OTHER TEAMS IN THE ORGANIZATION** | 107

A FINAL WORD | 113

ABOUT THE AUTHOR | 115

WHY YOU SHOULD
READ THIS BOOK

If I were to wish for anything, I should not wish for wealth and power, but for the passionate sense of the potential, for the eye which, ever young and ardent, sees the possible ... what wine is so sparkling, so fragrant, so intoxicating, as possibility!
—**Soren Kierkegaard,** *Danish Philosopher*

I have been a leadership and management consultant for over twenty-five years. A few years ago, I was happily consulting, being financially successful, loving my work, and seeing my clients' results. And then one day I heard someone say it was important to "give away what has been freely given to you," and I realized that I had been playing a small game. The work I was doing was making an impact, but we could only do it with a handful of companies at a time. I started to think about how I could substantially increase the impact we were having. I wanted to make a bigger difference in the world. So I began a three-fold approach: (1) expanding my own consulting practice; (2) training other consultants and consulting companies on the executive team alignment process and other consulting wisdom I might have; and (3) writing a book to reach others and give them a sense of what executive alignment is all about.

It is my belief that at some time in the not-too-distant future we will look back on this era as the dark ages of running companies. We will have discovered new ways of leading and managing and new ways of organizing. We will have unleashed human potential beyond anything we can now imagine, and as stunning as the new technologies that are developed will seem, it will pale in the light of what we realize about what people can do. We currently know a lot and we have evolved quite a bit, but in some areas we are fundamentally asleep as to what really is possible.

My own experience in the corporate world tells me that we need to go much further and that we have much greatness yet to reach. Executives spend much time, energy, and money on new strategies. Then they let these same strategies become mere shadows of what they originally envisioned through poor execution – not because they do not have the desire, the will, or the right people, but because they just have not developed an organizational culture of disciplined execution. CEOs pay little attention to the state of the executive team. In fact, calling most executive groups *teams* would be a stretch of the imagination since by definition a team is a group of people who are working on some common end together. And the idea that a group of executives are going to be able to achieve successful fulfillment without meaningfully engaging the next levels of leadership and the rest of the organization is ludicrous.

It is for the above reasons (and more) that management consultants are in business. No matter what, there will always be a need for outside help to be able to look at organizations and help executives lead and manage more effective companies. My own emphasis on executive team alignment and strategic implementation has enabled me to see many corporations from a close-up view, which has been both a privilege and an eye-opener. I am called in when a CEO has a particularly aggressive notion about where to take the company. Usually he or she is clear that to do it with the same tools and mindset that got them there is not going to work. There may have been a recent change in the executives or a re-structuring in the organization, and there is a desire to get the team clicking together quickly. Or, there is a new strategy (or a need for one), and getting the executive team to be aligned with it seems a daunting task. One CEO said to me, "You have what every CEO is looking for – a methodology for getting the people around him to understand and be a partner in the fulfillment of what he sees inside his own head."

Executive team alignment is one of seven pillars in the fulfillment of any strategic implementation, transformation, re-invention, or other significant organization-wide initiative. The executive team alignment process sets the foundation for the success of such implementation. The foundation (the process) covers at least three of the seven pillars. And when I use the term *pillar*, it means that without it, you and your team will fail or at least significantly dilute the impact of any initiative you take on.

I don't know of a more powerful organizational intervention than the executive team alignment process (ExecuTAP™ in my company). The ExecuTAP™ process has a basic design that is customized for every client situation. It is described in detail in this book. This process includes: several conversations with the CEO, president, or executive team leader to determine what accomplishment they are intending and what it means and what the apparent barriers are; one-on-one meetings with each of the team members to hear their points of view; usually two off-site sessions a few weeks apart to work the process together; follow-up meetings and coaching in between. I will discuss the benefits in depth as this little book proceeds, but suffice it to state for now that the end result will be an aligned, committed, executive team that is working together toward a compelling future that each person owns and can articulate, and they will at least have a high level plan for how they are going to get to that place. They will have a shared understanding of what it is going to take and a capability to sustain momentum. This is the foundation for a successful endeavor.

Every client has been extremely impressed and satisfied beyond their expectations. Implementing ExecuTAP always leads to breakthroughs in how the executives relate to the future of their company, their own roles in that future, and how to get there. When they are able to follow through with the fulfillment of the future they are creating, it has proven to be the foundation that can lead to phenomenal success.

The purpose of *The Transformational Power of Executive Team Alignment* is to give the reader a sense of what it is like to gain executive team alignment, why it is critical, and what is to be gained. Ultimately, my goal is to enable your organization to be as successful as you dream it can be and as great a company to be a part of as you can imagine. You owe it to yourself, your organization, or to your clients to find out how to make a huge difference in your success and the success of your enterprises. You may sense that your executive team is not very high performing. This book will help increase the potency of your executive team. You will learn more about something that is vital to the fulfillment of everything you aspire to have your company achieve.

You are embarking on a journey that could help you accomplish your highest aspirations for your organization. This is a beginning. I am reminded of taking a journey to some exotic tropical island. Perhaps that excursion begins with a click onto a website, reading descriptions of the amenities, perusing the photos, and finding out where the airports and the hotels are. Once you are satisfied that this is where you want to go, or at least you think it is but you need more information, you make the call or send the email that gets the ball rolling. And at the very least, you have enjoyed your little excursion mentally to the island, and it has helped you in some way to sort out where you want to go and even how to get there. Such is this journey into team alignment.

CHAPTER ONE

THE TRUTH ABOUT CURRENT

EXECUTIVE TEAMS

Life moves in one direction only –and each day we are faced with an actual set of circumstances, not with what might have been, not with what we might have done, but with what is, and with where we are now- and from this point we must proceed; not from where we were, not from where we wish we were - but from where we are.
—**Richard L. Evans**, *author, broadcaster, and church elder*

A TYPICAL EXECUTIVE TEAM

Everywhere I go, I find the problems that companies are struggling with are fascinating and the types of issues they face are common. When I have had the opportunity to explore further and to really look into the state of the executive team, I often see the same things. We have inherited an historical way of organizing and leading and interacting that has had us miss the real opportunities that leadership provides and that aligned executive teams might experience together.

And so there are a number of things I can state about executive teams that I have the audacity to believe fits a large percentage of them. I know there are exceptions, and if your team is one of those, then you will know what I am writing about and can attest to its veracity. It is what drives

me to want to get this process out more, because the result
of a relatively short immersion in a process like the one I
am describing has huge and long-lasting positive effects.

The typical team:

- Is a group of executives who meet once a week
  or less and talk about some issues and report on
  their divisional or departmental progress (or lack
  thereof)

- Is not a team at all, but closer to a committee

- Is not a <u>force</u> in the fulfillment of the company's
  vision and strategy, even though *individually* each
  member may be powerful and successful

- Is a group of people at least some of whom will
  say one thing in the meeting and a different thing
  in their minds (They will agree with the CEO
  by nodding their heads, but inside they are vig-
  orously shaking their heads and saying "Not on
  your life!")

- Spends a lot of time in meetings in conversations
  that often don't get them anywhere and do not
  turn into action

- Is one in which each member has his/her own agenda

Every week or every two weeks, this group gets together. There is an agenda for the meeting that they follow, although perhaps not very rigorously. At some point, some of them will report on the progress of his/her business unit or function, and occasionally other members will ask questions. Several business issues will be raised, most of them operational and not strategic, and if a decision is reached, the CEO or president will say, "Is everybody okay with that?" A couple of people will nod their heads and the meeting will proceed. Actually, others may not agree with the decision at all, but have given up on trying to fight that battle. A recurring sticky issue is brought up and the group will argue different perspectives on it for fifteen or twenty minutes, and finally the team leader will say, "enough," and they move on. At the end of the meeting, which has usually lasted a half hour or more later than was intended, there is little recap and each goes his or her separate ways, most (if not all) of them thinking, "I'm glad that's over."

The real tragedy here is that the highest paid people in the company have all come together for a substantial period of time and talked about things that are mostly non-strategic issues without meaningfully communicating with each other, without reaching many conclusions, rarely reaching any alignment, and without really "moving the ball forward" in the company. Each will fan out to the various departments and functional areas that they represent. If anyone asks about the meeting, they will say "Once again, we didn't accomplish much," or, "*They* decided so and so, but we're not going to pay much attention to that right now," implying that the executive team has done it again.

A TYPICAL EXECUTIVE

I define an executive as a person who is part of the lead group in an organization who has the accountability for overseeing the execution of the company's mission. In a corporation, an executive is usually an officer of the company with a fiduciary responsibility to the shareholders and a direct link to the board of directors.

These are intelligent people, skilled enough and persistent enough to have made it to the executive level. They are by and large good, honest, people who have been ambitious and committed enough to be where they are. They know what it takes to get ahead and they know something about leading others and motivating others to produce some level of results. But do they know how to participate fully and effectively as a team member among their peer teams?

As we have already explored, executive teams are typically not really teams and are not really a force for driving accomplishments within the organization. How would one describe a typical executive? How do they see their job and how they relate to other executives? How do they see their relationship to the fulfillment of the company's vision, mission, and strategy? I am not addressing here what they <u>think</u> about these aspects of their executive position, but instead what they expect when they come to work, what they actually do, what behaviors they exhibit, and what actions they take.

The typical executive:

- Does not have the faintest idea what the purpose of the team's getting together is. In fact few executive teams ever address the question "What is the purpose of this team, and what is the best bang for the buck in terms of our meeting?"

- Would rather eat razor blades than go to the executive "team" meetings. Of course this is not always the case. When I have one-on-one meetings with executives, I sometimes ask, "If we were old friends sitting in a bar and had a couple of drinks, and I asked you what you did today, and you said you went to an executive team meeting, and I asked how those were for you, what would you say?" The typical response ranges from "It's just something I have to do," or "Put it this way, it's not my favorite time of the week," to, "I sit there as patiently as I can waiting to get back to real work."

- Is not committed to the success of the other team members. In our competitive business environment, the competition often applies to how we relate to the people on our own team. One sometimes hopes others fail. At best, an executive knows that his teammate's success contributes to at least some aspect of his individual success (for instance, when an incentive bonus is connected to overall company targets), and he hopes that the other person is successful. But hoping someone is successful and actually being committed to that person's success are two completely different things.

- Is more interested in covering for himself or herself than in the effectiveness or impact of the meeting. An executive might have a hidden agenda to make sure that he/she looks good, or at least does not look bad. For example when he/she is reviewing progress toward certain targets, for this person would not tell the whole story, or not share concerns. Or, if the attention is on another teammate who is not doing well, he might be secretly satisfied that it isn't him/her on the hot seat, and also the longer he keeps attention focused on this other person, the more likely it is that they will not have the time to rip into him.

- Says *yes* when a decision is reached but often really means *NO*. He or she goes back to her division or business unit and says to her direct reports, "They decided to _____ but I am not in favor of it, so we'll just see how we can work around it," or "We'll just have to do the best we can under the circumstances." Perhaps they even ignore it completely.

If you add all of this together (and remember, I am asserting that this is typical), you end up with a team that is not at all cohesive, a team with individual agendas taking priority over team commitments, and with very little authentic conversation. Imagine what it would be like if a football team or a basketball team played that way. Do you think for one second that they would be successful, no matter how great the players themselves might be? It is doubtful. In the corporate world it is very much the same, except that a company could have a dysfunctional group like this forever, replacing individuals through attrition or otherwise, but always relating to each other in a similar manner. What is needed is an intervention, and the executive team alignment process is one such intervention.

THE TYPICAL CEO, PRESIDENT, OR OTHER SENIOR EXECUTIVE

And what about the CEO or whoever is accountable for the senior team? Let's refer to this person as the CEO. She has the ultimate accountability for the success of the enterprise. If the company does well, she will get the kudos (and the bonuses). If the company does not do well, she will get the blame, and eventually the boot. She has this lofty position because she is perceived as deserving and capable of doing a good job.

But does she have the level of skills needed for pulling a team of executive level people together and helping them to organize as a team by aligning, owning decisions and directions, and helping each other to be as successful as they can be? The evidence is that she does not know how to do this; otherwise, one would not find the typical condition so prevalent in corporations all over the world. CEOs are faced with awesome challenges and responsibilities, but where did they learn how to do this job? From experience, from others who have done it, from training they have had. But do they have the training that would bring together a team to have it be a real force in the fulfillment of the future that they are creating together? Again, the evidence says, no, they do not.

The typical CEO:

- Is relatively realistic about his team and how the typical executive on the team acts, but doesn't know what to do about it. He recognizes that team members have their own agendas, for example, and he attempts to have them transcend such limited vision. But he does not understand how to do this and rarely has a sufficient mentor.

- Would kill to be able to know that when an executive on the team says *yes*, he or she means *YES*. I have had many a CEO express to me some version of "If only...." One of the most common "if onlys" is this one: "If only my direct reports would really get what I envision and stand for it fully in the organization." Instead, what they end up with is a bunch of people who will pay lip service to decisions made or directions set, and then demonstrate unknowingly to the rest of the organization that there is no accord on the executive team. Thus, the CEO's vision is not satisfactorily being fulfilled.

- Craves that people around him will just be straight with him. It is another very common "if only": "If only people would just be straight with me." It is a need that a good consultant will often fulfill. The consultant may be the only person around a CEO who will go toe-to-toe with her client and will tell him the truth as she sees it.

- Wonders if she will ever be able to pull off what she would love to manifest if she only had the full support of her executive team. This is the deadliest aspect of having a team that is not as functional as it could be. It is a frustration that I have heard expressed by too many CEOs. It is often expressed as a request: "Can you help me get my people doing what I want them to do so that we can move toward what I see as possible in the future for this company?"

If you step back now and look at the typical executive team, the typical executive, and the typical CEO, it does not paint the prettiest of pictures. Keep in mind that these are all smart, talented, capable, people: proven leaders. But still they are stymied by how to pull everything together to get at least the foundation set for their companies to really soar.

THE CORPORATE ASPIRATION, OR THE CEO'S AGENDA

THE TEAM MEMBERS' AGENDAS

THE ALIGNED TEAM

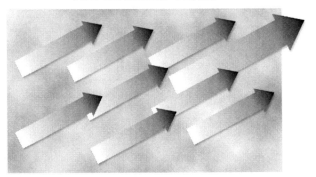

The solution to this "typical" dilemma is not all that difficult, but it takes some time and some skill to pull it off. The next chapter will begin to describe a process that has worked time and time again to take a typical team and a typical executive dilemma and build a strong, effective, aligned and committed team which is on a pathway to being a force in the company and fulfilling on some compelling future. Read on.

CHAPTER **TWO**

DEFINING

ALIGNMENT

Teamwork is the ability to work together toward a common vision. The ability to direct individual accomplishments toward organizational objectives. It is the fuel that allows common people to attain uncommon results.

—Andrew Carnegie

Alignment is a way to describe your relationship to decisions. This means that you have *a relationship to decisions whereby you own them completely.* There are many possibilities as to how you might relate to decisions. You might, for example, *agree* with them. If you agree with a decision, chances are you think it was the right decision and your relationship to that decision may be close to alignment. But not necessarily.

I say "close to" rather than "the same as" because agreeing with a decision does not necessitate that you own the decision completely. You could agree with a decision, say, to reduce the number of people in your company by 5%, and then go out and not participate in the process of staff reduction. There's nothing wrong with agreeing with a decision. In the best of all possible worlds, we would all 100% agree with every decision made that affects us personally or our company. But that's often not the case, is it?

Another relationship you might have to a decision is that you *disagree* with it. If you disagree with a decision, you probably are not going to own it and, in fact, you may be opposed to it. *Opposition* is another possible relationship to a decision that will negatively affect the outcome. So part of the problem with the paradigm of agreement/ disagreement is that you won't always agree, and disagreement breeds opposition. You might even resort to *resistance,* or even *sabotage.* In an extreme sense, any relationship to a decision that is not alignment could be said to potentially be a form of sabotage.

A vice president I will call Ron ran a business unit at a large manufacturing company. As part of the business planning process, a decision was made at an executive team session to reduce operating costs by 10% in the following year. Ron was a well-respected executive in the company, but when he left that particular meeting, he later admitted he was unsure of the wisdom of the decision because he did not think it was possible to reduce their costs that much in one year without destroying the company's ability to deliver the production performance required. He thought that if they reduced cost that much, it meant a reduction in staff. If they reduced their staff, they would cut into production. And if they cut into production, they would eliminate any savings from the cost reduction because their profits would be reduced due to production losses.

Ron might have been right, but he never brought that up in the meeting, and nobody else did either. So they walked out of the meeting with an *apparent* commitment to reduce costs in the next year. If they had known all of this, the result would have been predictable. What was the result? The following year, they reduced their costs by 5%, half of what their target was, and also had a significant loss in production that led to an overall loss of profitability. And Ron's unit was the weakest link in the chain.

The following year, this company went through an executive team alignment process. Ron saw what had happened the previous year and admitted it to the team. He saw that he had unknowingly sabotaged their efforts, and he committed to them that in the future he would fully express his concerns. That year, at a similar business planning session, a conversation began about reducing costs again. This time, Ron did voice his concern. "If we try to cut our costs by 10%, I am afraid that we will pay for it on the production end, and thus lose any profit benefit we would have gained," he said. This led to a very heated discussion and some more data gathering. In the end it was decided to reduce their costs by 5% and to find ways to *increase* their production sufficiently to more than make up for the additional 5% difference. The team committed to the results.

Ron came back to the executive team meeting a week later and shared what he had learned. "I left here committed to targets that I felt I had influenced, but I still did not know how we were going to achieve them in my unit. I got my team of managers together and I told them, 'This is what we committed to doing. Now, how are you going to accomplish it?' I met with each of them in the interim, and they told me what they thought each of them could accomplish. There was some nice dialogue and some impressing creativity. We now have a plan for achieving beyond what we thought was possible. I realize that when we did this a year ago, I wasn't aligned. I tried to reach the goals. But without that level of commitment, I had an excuse which was pretty much 'I tried and couldn't.' This time, I had no way out like that."

The result? Other team members took Ron's cue and worked in a similar manner with their respective teams. That next year, they met their reduction target and surpassed their production target by 10%, thus enjoying a profit margin that was tops in their industry. In addition, they used what they learned in increasing their productivity to continually improve on their production efficiency. Two years later they were expanding their capacity, hiring new employees, and benefiting from an excellent company culture.

OWNERSHIP

Alignment is a relationship to decisions where you own decisions as if they were yours. What does it mean "to own decisions?" I'm offering a different definition of ownership whereby it means *having something be yours completely, by choice.* You cannot force anyone to own anything. It has to be your choice. And you can choose to own things that are not formally or legally even yours (this is not an invitation to steal anything). You can "own" your child's school; that is, you can embrace it as your own, participate in it, volunteer for it, and represent it. People often own their city's sports teams. "This is my team," they say. That is a form of ownership by choice. It may not even be a fully conscious choice.

And you can legally own something that you don't "own" at all. An example might be a piece of property you inherited in another town that is just sitting there going to seed (or weed). You legally own it, but you do not own it in the sense we are using. You can, however, choose to own it, get it cleaned up and build on it, or sell it.

This is an important point because alignment must be by choice. You cannot force anyone to be aligned. That is *succumbing*, which is another possible relationship to a decision. All of these "relationships to decisions" are weak-

35

er than alignment. Alignment is the most powerful relationship you can have to a decision. And alignment is a choice.

As you may have gathered by now, there is a connection between alignment and commitment. In the next section we will explore that very important connection. The key to the benefit of alignment is in the commitments that go with it.

ALIGNMENT AND COMMITMENT

Alignment is also a *commitment to have a decision work*. If you are aligned, then you own the decision like it is yours and you are committed to making the decision work. It's important to remember that alignment is not a one-time thing. It must be able to be sustained over time. Think of it not as an event but as an ongoing commitment. An aligned executive team needs to be sure each team member is committed, which means that they will own every decision once it is made. Alignment is agreed upon as a team principle and is sustained over time.

You might think that an alternative would be to just seek alignment every time a decision is made. You can do that, but it does not give you an aligned team. What it gives you is a step above what you might have had before, which is the possibility of being aligned more often than not. But there is no guarantee. What happens if you make a decision and don't get alignment? Will you just step over the fact that you don't and go along as if you do? What does it mean when you don't have alignment? It means that at least one person on the team cannot own the decision. We have seen the consequences of this, so what will you do? And will you have to go through this every time a decision is made?

Executive team alignment is only powerful when it is a function of a commitment that has been made *in advance*. The commitment is this: Whenever a decision is made, I will align with it. This is radically different from anything most of us have participated in before, and there are implications. We will explore those later.

A second commitment that is part of alignment is to make a decision work. Once a decision is reached, you go out and do what the decision requires with an attitude of making it work. A company strategy, for example, is a series of decisions. It has been my observation that most companies make strategic decisions, do not reach alignment on them, and then the strategies fail to be implemented successfully.

I was introduced to the CEO of an electric utility company. This company had been successful in the past, but in the last few years had been failing to gain any new momentum and it was losing customers to its competitors. John, the CEO, told me that they developed new strategies with a lot of work, focus, and attention, but did not seem to be able to be successful with any of them. They wanted to make some acquisitions to expand their company services, but they were not finding the right purchases to make. When they did make a purchase, they struggled with getting them to be successful as part of their company. He said they now had another new strategy in which new acquisitions had much less of an emphasis, and he thought it would be a good strategy if they could somehow figure out how to pull this off successfully. When I asked him if his executive team was aligned, he replied, "That's the problem, I think!"

What I discovered in working further with this executive team was that they were very polite with each other but they also were very frustrated about their inability to successfully implement any strategy. In going through the process of their being an aligned team, it became evident that they did not even understand the new strategy and that they had some serious problems with the parts of it they thought they did understand. We ended up spending a lot of time just getting them to be able to have a shared understanding of the new strategy. When they did, they had even more problems with it. It became clear that they had downplayed the possibility of new acquisitions as a reaction to the past, but it was still their most viable and compelling strategy.

Most companies do not implement strategies well. In fact, many companies adopt strategies in concept, fail to implement successfully, and then ditch the strategy because they say it didn't work. Then, they create a new strategy, fail to successfully implement it, and then dump it. And on and on. I have a high regard for people who run companies because it is a very demanding and difficult job, but I also know that often the simplest and most rudimentary principles are not exercised.

ALIGNMENT IS AN INDIVIDUAL CAPABILITY

Alignment is a function of individual choices and individual capabilities. An aligned team is one in which the individuals have agreed to own every decision and to be committed to making the decisions and each other successful. As I've stated before, no one can be forced or coerced to align, at least not to be authentically aligned. It has to happen inside each person's heart as an act of will. If you have the individual capability to be aligned and stay aligned, and you are one of a team that has agreed to be an aligned team, then you will do whatever you have to do to get into alignment. Now that you have some basic understanding of alignment, ownership, and commitment, we can explore how they relate to executive team alignment.

EXECUTIVE TEAM ALIGNMENT

Having discussed alignment and what it is, ownership and commitment as they relate to alignment, and alignment as an individual capability, it is now time to pull it all together and discuss executive team alignment.

Executive team alignment is a phrase to describe leadership that is the driving force for the fulfillment of the enterprise's vision, mission, and strategy. They are truly performing their roles as *executives*, and they are *being a real team* – they are working together toward a common end. They have transformed themselves from a group of people with titles who get together and report to a team of executives who have real power.

They have chosen to be an aligned team. This choice is the transformational moment. And once they have chosen to be an aligned team they are stating both individually and as a group that they will own every decision with a commitment to have it work. They will move together as one body of people who demonstrate an authentic and sustainable commitment to the success of the enterprise.

I am not saying that the team reaches alignment after every decision. I am saying that once they agree to be an aligned team, they will be aligned to every decision. That is, once a decision is reached, they have agreed in advance to be aligned. The CEO does not ask after a decision is reached, "Are you aligned?" Rather, he or she *reminds* the team members that they have already agreed to be an aligned team, and may ask if anybody has any difficulty in owning the decision completely. If so, then he/she or the rest of the team can support that person in getting into full alignment. And this CEO may ask *before* the decision is reached if anybody would have any difficulty aligning on whatever the decision might be if, in fact, that decision is made. In other words, "After all of this discussion, I'm leaning toward saying 'yes' to this and I just wanted to see if I do make that decision, would anybody have any difficulty aligning with it?" This is just a way to check and perhaps uncover any last points that need discussion.

Think about that for a minute, because the implications are huge.

If you are going to be aligned with every decision, then that means you agree to align with decisions even when you *don't agree with them*. In other words, you agree to step off the right/wrong, agree/disagree continuum and choose to align regardless of where you happen to fall on that continuum. You can be completely "certain" that it is the wrong decision, yet you have agreed to align with it.

Is this a challenge? You bet. Whenever I've worked with executive teams on becoming an aligned team, when I get to this point, this becomes the subject of a good discussion. I'll often put this quote on the wall:

> *Beyond right and wrong,*
> *there is a field.*
> *I will meet you there.*
> **—Rumi, *Persian poet***

To be able to transcend your notion of agreement and disagreement and jump into the "field" where you can be aligned, regardless of whether or not you agree, is an extraordinary act. This is difficult for most people because we are not used to letting go of our points of view of right and wrong, or our personal notions of what is the best course of action. We are more used to holding on to these notions, without ever examining what the cost of such stubbornness might be.

I will often ask people who have difficulty with this conceptually, "Haven't you ever been wrong?" This will usually stop them in their tracks. And I will sometimes add, "Even when you *really* were sure you were right?" Of course they have. Sometimes I will add, "Today?" We all seem to have an investment in being right all the time, but a keen observer will conclude that many, if not most, of the day-to-day concepts that one thinks one is right about turns out to not be the case after all.

A mentor of mine used to ask, "Can you let go of thinking you are so smart that you know the right answer to everything?" Executives often believe that they are in the position they are in because of what they "know." But often leadership has more to do with the ability to "not know" than with the ability to "know." If you do not know, you have the opportunity to find out. If you think you already know, than what you call your knowledge is frozen in time. I am reminded of something philosopher Eric Hoffer said:

> In times of change, learners inherit the Earth, while the learned find themselves beautifully equipped to deal with a world that no longer exists.

It's important to point out here that we are not talking about sacrificing your values or your ethics. If a decision is reached that breaches your values or your ethics, you owe it to yourself and to the team to let them know that you cannot align. There will be consequences, of course, but they won't be as bad as you allowing your values or your ethics to be compromised. Think of what could have happened if someone at Enron, for example, had said, "No, I can't do that."

I have seen this happen only once. At a large corporation based in the Midwest, we had reached the point in working with the executive team that it was time for them to choose to be an aligned team. One of the dynamics involved in making that choice is that the team members must be sufficiently trusting of the CEO. There was one executive who had been with the company a long time who said no. He could not make that choice because he did not trust that the CEO would make decisions that were consistent with this person's values. After some dialogue, he also realized that his only choice was going to be to resign. He left the room with dignity. You may think this is a bad thing, but it changed this person's life for the better and stimulated a very meaningful conversation that made this a very strong team. It was an act of courage, and, in my opinion, was an example of the kind of integrity many companies and this world need.

To understand better what it means to be an aligned executive team, it is worth exploring what the benefits are. The following list is not in any particular order – all are significant benefits. It also is not necessarily an all inclusive list, but in my experience they are the top 10.

THE TOP 10 BENEFITS OF
EXECUTIVE TEAM ALIGNMENT

1. **Everyone on the team pulls in the same direction.**

   You are on a team where all are working toward the same vision and the fulfillment of the same strategy. When someone says "yes" to a decision in a meeting, he means "yes". If behaviors are observed later that seem to be counter to the commitment that the "yes" implied, then someone on the team will address those behaviors openly.

   The power of a team of people all pulling in the same direction cannot be overstated.

2. **There is a basis for sustaining momentum.**

   You can keep the energy and the momentum up because the team won't slow you down. Each team member owns the decisions and everyone is committed to achieve the goal. Members know what they need to do to keep themselves aligned. Because they are acting consistent with their commitments, they will be supported by others on the team.

45

3. **There is an element of certainty about successful implementation.**

You know that every team member wants to make the decision work and each member supports other members. You do not have the sense that some people have their own agendas. Implementation is not guaranteed, but the odds are more in your favor.

4. **There is a shift from an executive *group* to an executive *team*.**

The team is now a force that is running the company. The meetings are more meaningful and productive, and there is more trust. The CEO is no longer alone and he now has a key team of people thinking and acting from an enterprise-wide perspective.

5. **There is clarity around decision making.**

The team knows the decision-making process and each member does what he or she needs to do to support the process. There is less confusion about decisions that are reached and there is no longer any need to argue about decisions that are already made. (This does not mean that decisions can't be reconsidered – more about this later.)

6. **Decisions and implementation are made with greater speed.**

Although initial discussions might take some time, the team's ability overall to make decisions and move into action around them is much faster. Your ability to get into action as an organization has been greatly enhanced in terms of speed and quality of actions.

7. **If a better decision could have been reached, you are likely to know this much sooner.**

This may sound paradoxical at first, but if your organization makes a decision and is committed to make it work, you will know much sooner if it is not the best decision. The problem, as has been stated before, with many organizations is that they are so inconsistent in their implementation and execution that no one ever knows if the decision was a good one or not. After some time of poor execution, no strategic decision looks like a good one.

8. **Executives express themselves and contribute more.**

   Team members can be counted on to express themselves fully in pursuit of decisions, and thus they are more fully contributing what they have to contribute to the team. These are leadership traits, so one could easily say they are better leaders. They are also setting the example for the rest of the organization. Their decisions are more informed because of the quality and completeness of discussion around them.

9. **The executive aligned team is an example for the rest of the organization.**

   Nothing is more encouraging for the average employee in his or her hope for the future of the company than seeing that the executive team is aligned. There is also nothing more disruptive than not having an aligned team. Then the employees have to figure out where his or her allegiances lie and how to manipulate the system to survive.

10. **Being an aligned executive team creates the foundation for the success of the company.**

Again, executive team alignment is a critical success factor to the successful implementation of any company strategy or decision. Once you have alignment, the future of the company is now in the hands of a different entity than it was before: an aligned executive team, a force for the future of the enterprise. Being an aligned team and getting alignment can begin to be used at the next levels of leadership in the company, which then opens up the possibility that it can be used by all managers. You could end up with a truly aligned company!

WHAT ALIGNMENT IS NOT

- *Alignment is not consensus.* According to the dictionary, consensus means *the group as a whole agrees in the judgment or opinion.* In decision-making terms, consensus is a means of making a decision that requires everyone in the group to agree.

- Alignment is not a means of making a decision. There are many methods for making a decision, but alignment is not one of them. Alignment, as I am using the term, has to do with how one *relates* to decisions that are made no matter what method for making decisions is used.

- Alignment is not *"buying in."* The term *to buy in* is very popular in business these days. It is a pretty good thing to have people buy into ideas, but it is not as powerful as alignment. Would you rather have someone buy in to a strategy, or someone who owns the strategy completely?

CHAPTER THREE

KEY ELEMENTS OF A
SUCCESSFULLY ALIGNED TEAM

It is not because things are difficult that we do not dare; it is
because we do not dare that they are difficult.
—**Seneca,** *Roman rhetorician and writer*

It is critical to explore the many implications of being
an aligned executive team *before the team is asked to choose to*
be an aligned team. These are also key elements that make a
team successful in being aligned and sustaining that alignment. A team can keep its commitment and success going
over time by checking for each of these elements often.

A SHARED UNDERSTANDING OF ALIGNMENT

To be an aligned team, there needs to be a shared
understanding of what is meant by alignment. People often have different ideas of exactly what this concept means.
I have worked with CEOs who have claimed to have an
aligned team (it is very rare that they will even say that),
but when I asked the individuals on the team to tell me
what alignment meant, each and every one of them did
some version of scratching their heads and saying, "Hmm,
I never even thought about what it means." Were they
aligned? Absolutely not!

It is imperative that there is an in-depth discussion
about what alignment is and what it implies. The discus-

sions themselves produce value even beyond the act of aligning because of the conversations that arise. These discussions can trigger revealing attitudes, beliefs, opinions, and habits of the team members.

We worked with a Canadian oil company that had enjoyed a degree of success in the past. We were discussing how to define alignment that makes it the most practically useful, and we had gotten to the part of the discussion that had to do with being committed to each other's success. Harry, who was the vice president in charge of exploration, started a conversation that went something like this:

"In my end of the business, I am the expert, and that's why I'm in this position. I fail more than I succeed because few of the potential sites I explore turn out to be worth investing in drilling. In order to be successful enough, I need to get to the yes/no decision quickly so I can get to the ones that are going to yield oil to us quickly. What I don't want are a bunch of non-geologists bothering me with questions and interest in what I am doing that is going to contribute to nothing but slowing me down."

There was some discussion about this and then I said, "I'm sure that everyone in here hopes you are successful, am I right?" There was much nodding of heads. "If you are not successful, then the company is not successful, and everyone in here will at least bear the brunt of some of that, right?" More assent. "But what difference could it make if each person on this team was *committed* to your success versus simply *hoping* that you were going to be successful?"

Sharon, the head of drilling operations, raised her hand. "Because of the nature of the drilling cycle, I sometimes have employees who could be temporarily utilized elsewhere. Suppose I made them available to you when the adding of more workers could make a difference in the time it takes you to make a decision about the site you are exploring?"

Joseph, the CFO added: "And we could find a way to compensate any employees who make themselves available for this kind of temporary duty. This would likely accelerate the possibility of their availability without sacrificing anything on the drilling operations end."

Thomas, the senior vice president of HR said: "I don't need to get into the details of what it takes to assess a possible site or anything else that has to do with your job, Harry. But there are things I see I could do to help that I haven't even thought of before, and I'm beginning to hear things that could move me from 'hoping' you'd be successful to betting that you would be."

And the conversation continued. In a period of maybe ten minutes it became clear that the pervading attitude had been one of independence and isolation from others, and everyone could see the benefit of moving to interdependence and partnership with others. By the way, in the following year this company significantly outperformed anyone's predictions.

The value of these kinds of revelations is what makes the executive team alignment process so impactful. In the previous example, whole new worlds of possibility emerged from a very basic discussion stimulated by simply defining alignment, which, in turn, made a tremendous difference in the long-term performance of the company.

AN UNDERSTANDING OF THE DECISION-MAKING PROCESS

Another responsibility of being part of an aligned team is to really have an understanding of the decision-making process – who makes the decisions and how they are made. If you are going to be part of an aligned team, which means you are going to own every decision that is reached, the first thing you'd want to know is who makes the decisions and how they are made.

On an executive team, the CEO or the president (or whatever the designation of the top team member) is accountable for the success of the team and typically has the ultimate decision-making authority. There are a number of ways that he or she may go about the process of making that decision. The following are some of those key ways:

- **Directive** – The leader makes the decisions and informs the team.

- **Testing** – The leader makes the decision and then tests it with the team before finalizing it.

- **Consulting** – The leader leads a discussion with his team and at some point will make the decision based on the information.

- **Delegating** – A small group is given the task of making the decision.

- **Voting** – The majority or some percentage of the group decides.

- **Getting consensus** – Every person on the team needs to agree to the decision for it to be made.

The above list represents the most common methods. Each of these can be used effectively and each has its own advantages and disadvantages. Some are more conducive to being effective in certain situations than others. Getting consensus is too slow for most businesses, but works very well for more community-oriented organizations. Voting works for democracies, but not much for businesses where the majority may not have all of the information or training required to be able know which way to vote. The directive method may be critical in emergency situations, but most CEOs in today's corporate world do not use this method to the exclusion of others.

The important thing is that the team knows what method is being used so that the members can make informed choices about being an aligned team and can understand the implications. It is possible that you would not choose to be an aligned team member if you find out , for example, that decisions are reached on the team completely by the directive method, and you do not have the confidence in the CEO to honestly be aligned on all decisions. I have found that most senior leaders use a combination of the methods. They see if they can get consensus, and if they don't they make the decision themselves at some point. Sometimes they test the decision, but often they need to make decisions without being able to consult with the team first.

Franklin was the president of a financial services company in Maryland. He was one of the best and most compassionate leaders I have ever worked with. His leadership style was very engaging and he was committed to having his company maximize its possibility as a great place to work through giving each person respect, authority to make decisions, and creative license within limits.

When I asked Franklin what his decision-making process was before the team session, he told me it was to gain consensus. I took it at face value for the moment even though I knew it was unlikely that this was really true. It was not that Franklin was purposefully telling an untruth; rather, he was more than likely not really aware fully of what his decision-making process was. At the executive team alignment session that followed, the discussion among the team members revealed to Franklin what he could not easily see for himself.

His first realization was that, yes, he preferred to gain what he called consensus (he looked around the room and if most people were nodding their heads, he assumed he had everybody on board), but when this version of consensus was not really forthcoming, then he made the decision himself. In fact, most of the time he made the decision himself. How did he come to this realization? When I talked about the different decision-making process choices and I asked him again what his preferred method was, he said again that it was consensus. There was a moment of silence and then one person said, "Franklin, in all due respect, that isn't true! You seem to search for consensus, but more often than not you talk about it for a while and then make the decision." From the nodding of the heads in the room, now Franklin had to reflect on the veracity of the statement. And he saw it was true.

"I guess I use more of a consulting method than I thought," Franklin said.

Another person added, "Well, now that I think about it, I think you use the consulting method sometimes, but I also think you use the testing method sometimes, too." Franklin thought back to what actually happened when he was trying to reach a decision in a team meeting, and he could see that this was the case. He would sometimes come into the conversation in order to get the team's input in order to make the best decision, and other times he already knew pretty much what the decision was going to be, and he was just testing to see if he made that decision what the reaction was going to be (realization #2). But he wasn't done.

"You know," piped up another team member, "I don't have any problem with your seeking consensus as a preference, and then making the decision yourself when it is required. I think it's your prerogative and not a bad way to go. But I have a request: When you are testing a decision, say so, and when you are consulting us on a decision, say that. In other words, let us know what the method is that you are using. The reason I am asking for this is that it tells me how to participate in the conversation and it doesn't set me up for an expectation that will not be fulfilled."

Franklin's third realization in this discussion was that when he tests a decision with the team and they think he is looking for input to *determine* his decision, then they are responding in a way that they anticipate will help him make the decision. But when they realize that he was really just testing a decision already made, they feel a little bit foolish and as if they had been duped. It was not giving them the respect that he had intended to always give them. He accepted their request with one condition. "I agree to let you know beforehand which method I am using, but I am not practiced at this. So if you are in doubt as to which method is being used and I haven't stated it, will you stop me and ask?" The team agreed.

Franklin's desire to have a great company in which to work took a tremendous leap forward with this one conversation. The executives felt more empowered and trusted. They were able to begin to be more effective at imparting that same empowerment to the people they managed. Their foundation for success had just added another pillar.

I have found that most senior executives gravitate to a mixed method of making decisions, and I have come to believe that a mixture is best. As the example with Franklin demonstrates, there are some pitfalls, and the most common is that you need to be clear with your people which method you are using. One client I had in a Scandinavian country insisted that his methodology was going to always be consensus. I usually do not interfere with a leader's choice in how they will make decisions – I will inform them of the other possible choices only – but this time I felt I had to let him know that insisting that you always have complete consensus was impractical. He heard what I had to say, and then he reiterated that this was how he intended to do things. About a month later, he called me to tell me that he was now including other methods because if he relied solely on consensus, it was taking too long to reach decisions.

Also, the team must understand that they will not be able to be part of every decision that is made. Sometimes the team leader must make a decision without involving his team – either the decision must be made on the spot or there are sensitivities around the decision that can't be shared with the whole team. A CEO might need to make a momentary decision at a board meeting, for example. Typically, personnel decisions about needing to make a change on the executive team are made privately, separate from the

KEY ELEMENTS OF A SUCCESSFULLY ALIGNED TEAM

rest of the team. This need to make some decisions without including the rest of the team presents another big challenge. These challenges must be dealt with as part of the discussion on becoming an aligned team. An aligned executive team must be willing to be aligned with decisions *whether they are part of the decisions or not.* In other words, they must be able to own decisions that are made with or without their participation or input in them.

Being clear about the decision-making process on an executive team is critical to the success of the team and to the process of choosing to be an aligned team. First, to be able to make the choice to be an aligned team, you need to know what that decision-making process is because this information could be important to your making that choice or not. Second, and probably more important, is the quality of discussions, revelations, and realizations that often occur during the course of the conversation about decision making. When I conduct a decision-making session with an executive team, I always make time allowances for the likelihood that some significant and useful dialogue could occur during this discussion. Although it could take an hour, it could also take four hours. And if it does, it is four hours well worth it.

And why is it worth it? Because the real "gold" in this executive team alignment process is not what the facilitator plans or says, but in what emerges in terms of straight talk in the team discussions. Straight talk is defined here as *saying what needs to be said in order to increase the likelihood that the discussion is of value and reaches the most useful conclusion*. When executive team members can be counted on to be straight with each other, they are fulfilling a critical requirement for being successful.

SAYING WHAT NEEDS TO BE SAID

Another key element of being part of an aligned executive team is that when you are a team member in the decision-making or discussion process, you must be willing to say what needs to be said while you have the opportunity. If you hold back and don't say what you see or what you think and a decision goes against what you thought, then you are guilty by omission. It will be more difficult for you to authentically align with your team.

You must be willing to champion your point of view. This might even mean arguing for an unpopular perspective or disagreeing openly with a CEO or a friend on the team. You must be willing to go to bat for what you think is right *while the discussion is open and on the table and before the decision is reached*. Remember that once the decision is reached, you have committed to aligning with it whether you agree with the decision or not.

Saying what needs to be said requires *honesty and openness*, which is the willingness to say what needs to be said. This honesty also implies that you are more committed to contributing to the thinking that goes into the ultimate decision than you are to looking good, being politically correct, being polite, or being safe. *Honesty is not an excuse for being stupid*, though. You should always be your own judge about how much can be said, how hard to play it, or how long to take a position. If, for example, you can sense that you have made your point as fully as it can be made, and that by continuing to argue that point will only alienate the other team members, then it is time to stop. In addition, it is one thing to express your point of view and another to just appear to be argumentative. This is not about being argumentative for its own sake – it is about saying what needs to be said to move the ball forward.

You do not need to risk your job by saying what needs to be said. I have been at very few companies where people actually got fired because they had a different perspective on something. Executives are usually mature enough to want to hear opposing points of view. I will sometimes ask people one-on-one (when I know they are not forthcoming about something) what they perceive as the consequence. "I will make Beatrice angry," they will sometimes answer.

"And if Beatrice gets angry, then what?" I ask. "Then she gets angry, that's all." Everyone gets angry sometimes, and executives cannot afford to refrain from saying what needs to be said to avoid their CEO's anger. You have to be the judge of when and where to say anything that you suspect will trigger an angry response.

One company I worked with in Texas had an executive team that was expressing itself more and more but still had moments where it would shut down. At an executive team meeting that I attended as a coach, the CEO's face got red and he started to yell angrily about something that was said. Everything got very quiet for a minute, and then the meeting proceeded. But it had clearly shut down. "What just happened?" I asked.

Finally someone answered, "Michael got angry at something Deborah said, and it shut us all up."

I said, "Michael, do you get angry sometimes?"

"Of course," he answered.

"Is it okay with you if you get angry sometimes?"

"Yes."

"Do you come to any conclusions about the people who triggered your anger?"

"No. I get angry sometimes, and I shouldn't. But I do, and it has nothing to do with the person who said whatever they said."

I then addressed the team: "Michael gets angry sometimes. He does not then make a note of who said what and hold it against that person. He gets over it, and it is okay with him to get angry sometimes, although he'd rather he was a more mild-mannered person. Now, can you allow him to be angry when he gets angry?" Everyone said they could. "And can you be willing to trigger his anger from time to time and not be stopped by it?" They said they could, and although it is naïve to think this one conversation was the complete cure, they were a much transformed team after that, being more consistently open and straight with each other and less likely to be reactive to the CEO's occasional angry outbursts.

The point is to be courageous enough to get into the fray and contribute as much as possible to reach an informed decision-making stage. Every senior executive I have ever met has told me that this is what he or she wants from their teams. One of the major benefits of being and staying an aligned team is that it requires behaviors that strengthen the team and the company. Setting the example by saying what needs to be said to the executive team goes a long way toward creating a culture of straight talk, which in turn becomes not only a culture that is healthy and inspiring but also sets the stage for powerful execution and performance.

BEING COMMITTED TO EACH OTHER'S SUCCESS

We've already discussed committing to alignment, but that was more about committing to the alignment process as a whole. It's also important to commit to your team members. If alignment means ownership, then the executive team is now a team of co-owners – or, in other words, partners. Being a partner means you must be as committed to your partners' success as you are to your own – if fact, their success *is* your success, and vice versa. If you each own the strategy, then each of you must be committed to fulfilling your part of the strategy and to supporting each other's successes their parts.

Why is this different? Most often, different executive team members do not relate to each other as committed partners in the fulfillment of the vision and the strategy. More than likely, they are either "on your side" – that is they hope you will be successful at what you do, because it will mean the company will be more likely to be successful – or they will consider you a barrier to their own success and will not be in favor of your success at all. (This latter is more often than not unconscious.)

Let's look at an example. Imagine you are the head of a business unit that manufactures widgets and your unit contributes 20% of the gross profits of the company. Judy is the head of another business unit that manufactures wobbets, and they contribute another 20% of the profits. You think Judy is okay, and you would like her to be successful, especially since your compensation is 50% based upon the total company profits, so the more successful Judy is the more successful you are. But, of course, you can be successful without her being successful, even if it would be better if she were. Your attitude and your behavior towards her in your executive team meetings can be summed up as: "I hope you are successful."

Herbert, however, is the Senior Vice President of Human Resources. Herbert is a good enough guy, but you think Human Resources is overly process-oriented, too demanding for a function that does not contribute to the profits of the company, and is a source of too much corporate expense which takes away from your bottom line. You have no interest in Herbert's success. You'd rather he just left you and your unit alone. Your attitude toward him in your executive team meetings might be summarized as: "Just go away and leave us adults alone."

Now, what happens when you are an aligned team? One of the things you come to realize is that both Judy and Herbert are your partners, and their success is your success, and you are now committed to their being successful. For Judy, this may mean asking her questions about how things are going in her unit, finding out more of the details (not prying into her business but being supportive of her), and seeing if there is anything you can contribute. Your attitude is "You are my partner and I am committed to your success."

With Herbert, you realize that he is your partner and you must be committed to his success as well. If you think about it, you know that HR is very critical to the success of your unit (and Judy's), that it helps you hire new people, keep the ones you have, and handle all of their compensation and benefits. It is, in fact, a supportive function to you. If it isn't working well, then it isn't giving you the maximum support you need. By your commitment to Herbert you can help him have the strongest supportive function possible. Perhaps you can ask him to meet with you to openly discuss what seems to be working and not working about his functional unit in an effort to make it better. Now your attitude is "You are my partner and I am committed to your success."

You want to try and extend this to every member of your executive team. Then it really becomes a team and the possibilities are endless. Your executive team meetings can begin to become meaningful because you are all working toward the same end as team members and as partners.

ADDITIONAL ASPECTS OF BEING AN EFFECTIVE ALIGNED TEAM MEMBER

- Be responsible for understanding the issues before a decision is reached. If you don't understand something, ask about it even if you feel stupid not knowing. One trick I use is that I tell myself that if I don't understand something, my asking might be a contribution to others.

- A corollary to this is to make sure there is a shared understanding of something when it is not obvious. We are always assuming, for instance, that we have the same understanding of words we use (like alignment), but quite often we don't. Develop the good habit of questioning what people mean when they use words that could have different meanings.

- Once the decision is made, make sure that whenever you say something about it, you are representing your alignment. There is no "they" when talking about who made the decision. In fact, be cautious even saying "we," because you may be avoiding responsibility. You must own the decision no matter how it's made. It appears to be human nature to second-guess even our own decisions, and even more subtle is our tendency to downplay a decisive act. An example of this is by saying "Yeah, I guess we did say that, but..." diminishes the power of the team, of being aligned, and of the decision reached.

- As a member of an aligned team, you have the responsibility to make sure you are informed about the issues being discussed. This may mean knowing beforehand what issue is going to be discussed and doing your homework so you are prepared to discuss it. Ignorance is not an excuse for making bad decisions or for not being able to align on decisions made.

- Express your point of view while the issue is being discussed and do not be too quick to give it up if there still seems to be value in taking that position.

Remember to be willing to let go once the decision is reached. If you feel strongly that xyz is the right way to go but the decision turns out to be zxy, then drop your position and own zxy. This will be very difficult if you are not used to it, but it will reward you in many ways. Again, I often ask people, "Weren't you ever wrong? In fact, haven't you ever felt very strongly about something only to find out it wasn't the way you thought it was going to be?"

CHAPTER **FOUR**

SUSTAINING

ALIGNMENT

SUSTAINING ALIGNMENT

Unless one is committed, there is hesitancy, the chance to draw
back, always ineffectiveness. Concerning all acts of initiative there
is one elementary truth, the ignorance of which kills countless
ideas and endless plans: That the moment one definitely commits
oneself, then providence moves, too.

—Goethe, *German poet, playwright, and philosopher*

Sustaining alignment will be a challenge. Maintaining any new behavior is a challenge, and being an aligned team requires many new behaviors that may seem counterintuitive to the way you live. If executive team alignment sessions are effective, then people come out of them inspired, energized, and committed. But then sometimes Monday morning comes around and "business as usual" tends to put a dent in their enthusiasm.

For example, on Friday you were committed to each other's success, but on Monday there was an injury on the floor at one of the manufacturing plants, and you immediately resorted to your old behavior of blaming the vice president in charge rather than seeing if you can support her in any way in dealing with the crisis and improving safety measures. You found out that the CEO has fired your friend, the VP of Marketing, and you react very negatively to this decision and swear you will never allow yourself to be sucked into being aligned again. You get the monthly

77

financials and there is an obvious downward trend in revenues that is unexpected, and you say to yourself, "To hell with the new strategy, we need to focus on cash coming in!" These are understandable reactions to what happens on a day-to-day basis in the life of an executive, and they present the biggest challenge to sustaining alignment. The *drift* – the direction the flow of things seems to be going when intentionality is not present – is toward dropping the drive to the future and just dealing with the fires that need to be put out. The momentum that had been created has now dissipated.

To get the most out of this section, do not limit yourself to reading only those passages that seem to deal with you in your position. If you are the CEO, read the section that is for the executive team member as well. It is equally important for you to be the leader of sustaining alignment. If you are a team member, read the section for the CEO. A lot of it applies to you as well, and, more importantly, this is critical for you to be a partner to the CEO in keeping the team aligned and supporting the CEO.

I have had the privilege of working with clients intimately and for relatively long periods of time and I have been through the whole cycle enough times to know where the pitfalls are. I have seen over and over again how much repetition is needed for new behaviors to become habitual and for commitments made to be re-energized. If you consider how difficult it is for most people to turn New Year's resolutions into real commitments that they keep alive, multiply this tenfold and you begin to see the enormity of the task for an executive team.

I state this as a *caveat*. Do not despair. It is the challenge all organizations must face in order to get better and better at moving toward a compelling future that they have created. It is what takes an enterprise out of the drift and into some momentum in new directions. It is a not only a worthy undertaking, but perhaps the most meaningful one you can take on. John F. Kennedy said the following, and it applies beautifully to this exciting adventure:

> *We choose to go to the moon in this decade and do the other things, not because they are easy, but because they are hard. Because that goal will serve to organize and measure the best of our energies and skills. Because that challenge is one that we are willing to accept, one that we are unwilling to postpone and one that we intend to win.*

In order to assist you in sustaining alignment and being successful at your version of going "to the moon," consider the following advice.

FOR THE CEO

As I'm sure you're aware, sustaining an aligned team takes skill and attention. Being an aligned executive team is not a one-time event. It is an ongoing journey. Being the CEO, you want to make sure that your team is willing and able to stay aligned. Because they are part of the aligned team, you can be assured that *they have made that commitment, and you can hold them to their word.* It is your responsibility to have faith that they are committed even though you may have to remind them when they are off track.

Committing to being aligned should not be treated the same way we usually treat New Year's resolutions. Like many people, I typically make my New Year's resolutions on New Year's Eve. If my resolutions last a week I'm surprised. By the end of January I usually forget which resolutions I had chosen.

A commitment made to self and others is a different matter. I am a stickler for being clear about the difference between simply thinking I would like to do something and actually making commitments and keeping those commitments. But I slip sometimes, and so do you. Part of the challenge of keeping commitments is sticking to them even when your mind says not to or when your will weakens. And this is true for your executive team members as well.

We can all "build this muscle," but in the meantime, part of your job as the CEO is to hold your team to their commitments and remind them when they need reminding.

I once worked with the executive team of a food manufacturing company committed to increasing their existing distribution channels and increasing their sales within a year by a whopping 25%. It seemed a lofty goal, but was not impossible since the company really had not expanded their distribution possibilities in many years. The early stage of their plan for moving forward was to test a list of potential distribution alternatives to see what kind of resistance they might meet by existing channels. Then they would determine how to minimize any negative impact and to evaluate the options or trade-offs.

As they were completing this stage, they could see that two of their potential new channels had huge upside potential and only one of them could have any significant downside, but even that one could be managed. The likelihood that they could be successful at developing these channels was very high. Meanwhile, unknown to the rest of the team, the CEO had been asked to meet with a chief executive of another food manufacturing company who subsequently made an offer to buy my client's company. After much discussion and negotiation with the proper stakeholders and interested parties, the offer was officially tendered and a conditional acceptance was signed. Then it became public knowledge.

The executive team was shocked. They had been a fiercely independent culture and were shaken by the notion that they were going to be sold. Their very jobs were threatened. After a very open and robust meeting, they saw the rationale for the sale and the wisdom of it from the point of view of their fiduciary responsibility to their shareholders. No one could argue the logic of it. They still had their individual concerns, but they could maintain their alignment even in the face of their being acquired.

The fulfillment of their strategy at this point was another challenge altogether. No one seemed to have any energy concerning the pursuit of their new distribution channel ideas. What was the use? They were going to be bought, anyway, and no telling what the new entity would adopt as a strategy.

The CEO stepped up to the challenge. "We will proceed as planned," he said. "No matter what happens, we can only benefit by being successful at the strategy we began when we all were together a few months ago. This is an understandable bump on the road, but we must not let it stop us. I cannot imagine any configurations of future leadership teams who wouldn't benefit and celebrate a 25% increase in revenue. Let's keep going!"

And they stepped up to renewing their challenge. Within a short period of time and while the discussion to close the deal were still going on, the company began the work needed to make the two new channels a reality. As it turned out, the deal died. But their energy toward being an aligned team committed to the future they created did not, and the company met its revenue targets in that next year. Their stock, by the way, increased more than the sale of the company was likely to yield.

As you well know by now, executive team alignment is a commitment to being aligned to decisions once they are made; to doing what you have to do to be an active part of the process when you can; to owning decisions once they are reached as if they are yours; to making the decisions work; and to the success of each of the team members. For the most part, all of this is new behavior and we do not change overnight. It takes practice and it takes support from others.

Here are some guidelines that might be helpful:

- When a decision is reached in a meeting, ac-knowledge that a decision has been made and repeat what it is. Ask if there are any questions about it. Remind people that from this moment on, they have already agreed to own this decision completely. You can even go around the room and ask for a nod of the head if this is understood, or, if there is any problem with it, to speak up now. It is useful to do that a few times in the beginning, and then occasionally thereafter.

- If you observe anyone speaking negatively or irresponsibly about a decision that was reached, remind them that this is not acting consistently with the commitment. Do not chastise. This person has made a commitment that requires a change in behavior, and he or she will slip from time to time.

- Do not assume that because someone is not acting consistent with their commitment that he didn't mean it. He said it; he meant it (that's what you assume). If you act as if people did not mean their commitments, then the commitments will disappear. If you act as if they did mean them, then their commitments will stay alive.

- Test a decision just before you are ready to make it. Ask, "If I (or we) make this decision, would anyone here have difficulty aligning with it?" And then look for their responses. If someone says they are having difficulty aligning, ask why. Listen to the response and unless the reason alters your pending decision, tell him you understand his concern but after consideration, you are still likely to make that same decision. And acknowledge his being willing to speak out and being willing to align even when it is difficult. Remind the team that to be an aligned team requires some personal challenges, but it is worth it.

- Seek people out individually (not in the team meeting) if their behavior is often inconsistent with being aligned. Again, chastising is probably not the best way to get their alignment. Be as helpful and understanding as you can, but be clear with them that what you expect is that they will keep their word and be aligned. If they cannot do it, then at some point you will need to find someone who can. If this seems harsh, think about the consequences of not being aligned. Do you want an executive on your team who cannot consistently align? Someone who cannot own the decision and will not be committed to making it work?

FOR THE TEAM MEMBER

Although the CEO is ultimately accountable for the success of the enterprise as well as the success of his team, as his "partner" each and every executive has a huge stake in the game and can and must play as big a role in the team's success as possible. If you think of yourself as the CEO's partner, you will act differently than if you think of yourself a passive receiver of hierarchical direction. It can be said that you are a leader because of your willingness to be responsible for creating the future. This is a proactive and full commitment that needs to be operative in every aspect of your work. Sustaining alignment requires this degree of ownership as well.

Here are some tips that apply to every team member:

- Monitor your own speaking in your own unit or department. Be responsible for speaking in a way that represents your ownership of the decisions. When you catch yourself slipping (and you will), clean it up.

- Coach others when they slip. Just let them know that you observed them speaking or acting in a way that is inconsistent with being an aligned team member. As their partner, you want to remind them of the commitment everyone made. You can share with them that you've found yourself doing the same thing (if this is true), but that everyone needs to help each other be successful. Do not get self-righteous about their slip. That will have the opposite effect.

- Be true to yourself in the executive team meetings. Remember, ultimately alignment is an individual capability, and only you knows what is going on inside yourself. Speak your mind. Say what needs to be said. And when it's time to let go, do it.

- If your CEO is not managing the sustaining of alignment, consider talking to him or her about it. You have to be the judge of how to best do this. If you can't and there is not someone else on the team who can, the team is in trouble. Most likely, the best approach is to ask for private time with the CEO. When you get it, tell this person that this conversation the two of you are having is in the context of the fulfillment of the team's commitment to the vision, and that you are seeing behavior on his/her part that appears to be counter to the commitment to being an aligned team.

- As mentioned earlier, when a decision is reached, make sure that you understand exactly what the decision is and what it means. Ask for clarification if you are not certain.

- Watch to see that you are staying true to being committed to each team member's success. If this means getting together with one or more of them and discussing things, then so be it. The biggest outcome from all of this is what will happen when you have formulated your partnerships with each of the team members.

CHAPTER **FIVE**

GETTING INTO ACTION NOW

WHAT TO DO UNTIL THE DOCTOR
COMES (SO TO SPEAK)

Everything that I have written in the pages preceding this chapter has assumed that it would be useful to know what executive team alignment is all about, to understand what it is going to take and what the benefits are. I would hope that by now you are clear about the benefits and you are all for getting them.

I also assumed that in order to have an aligned team in the way I have described it, you need an outside person (a trained consultant) to help you with this. I have always told people that there is no way they can do this themselves, and there is even very little chance that they could have an internal person facilitate it. I have already expressed what the difficulty is: suffice it to say that without an external person to help you, you will run into the very same dynamic that keeps things in place as they are. If team members have been unwilling to tell the truth before, for example, what will get them to begin to tell it now?

However, I would like to leave every reader with some actions they can take. In a way, it is similar to "what to do until the doctor comes", but I'm not crazy about the analogy because I am not crazy about someone on an executive team thinking in terms of sickness. Sickness is an aberration, and there is nothing aberrant about executives that are not aligned. It is very normal, if not ideal. And, although I am cautious about the likelihood of a company's being able to pull this off without help, I would certainly support it.

One more thing: what is in this chapter is not just what to do if you are not going to hire a consultant; *it is also what to do even after you have your aligned team in place.*

No matter where you sit on a team – whether you are the team leader or simply a team member – there are things that you can do to move the team forward in terms of being an aligned team. It takes time and patience, and there is no guarantee that you will get there. It takes leadership, if leadership implies you will be the example and influence people in a direction. I say it does include that.

It boils down to this: *How do you as an individual contribute to a team's moving closer and closer to being an aligned team?* Which could be said as, *how do you contribute to your team's success?*

Of course, there are other factors that contribute to a team's success in addition to being an aligned team, but alignment is the first, most basic and fundamental requirement for a successful team. Here are some of the additional factors (in no particular order):

1. **Relationship with each other**

   Do team member respect each other? Do they generally like each other enough to work effectively with them?

2. **Trust**

   Do people trust each other in the ways that are important for them to be able to work effectively together? In other words, do they trust that they will do what they say they do, that they will tell the truth, that they are sufficiently knowledgeable and capable in their area, that they will be loyal, etc.?

3. **There is some synergy of capabilities and tendencies**

   Not everybody has to be perfect at everything, but together the team complements each other in a way that makes for a smooth and complete working possibility.

4. **People listen to each other**

   This is related to all of the above bullets, but deserves one of its own. If team members listen to

each other, then each has an opportunity to contribute to the whole.

5. **Time together as a team is time well spent**

Meetings move along and are meaningful. The
agendas are scrubbed for appropriate content,
asking, 'Is this something this group needs to discuss?' Decisions that are made are noted. Conversations move into future actions, and actions are
recorded and tracked.

6. **Straight talk**

Whether your team is aligned or not, straight
talk is always a quality and a willingness of team
members to say what needs to be said and not
hold back (and do it skillfully, I might add).

You may have already realized that almost any trait
you can attribute to a high-performance team is related to a
requirement for being an aligned team. That is, the process
of aligning a team covers to some degree each of the above-
listed factors. This will also perhaps give you a hint on how
to move your team toward being an aligned one over time.
In a way, it is working upside-down from the process I have
previously described. If you are going to try and do it yourself, or at least improve the quality of your team, you have

to work on yourself and the team's developing the traits of an aligned team.

I do not mean to make light of any of the factors listed above. Each is significant. I could write another book about trust in the organizational setting, for example. I have spent many hours helping especially executive teams have more effective meetings (and more effective action between meetings). I merely want to point out that (1) there are many other factors that go into high-performance teams and (2) the team alignment process will cover many of these, at least as a beginning approach to them.

SO WHAT DO YOU DO?

I mean to underscore the *you* here. *You* as in you, the person reading this. This part is about what you can do as an individual to lead by example in supporting the team in moving towards being an aligned team. This is not what you can ask or support or suggest what others ought to do. I'll get to that. This is about what you could do, quietly and unobtrusively and, perhaps, without ever drawing attention to yourself or getting acknowledged or recognized for it.

In no particular order:

1. Align. That is, when a decision is reached on your team, choose to own it, to being committed to make it work, and to always speak consistent with this commitment. Do not wait for it to be proven out; do not wait for the decision to change; do not (DO NOT) refer to it as "his" or "her" decision and "we have to live with it". Simply align with it.

    - This sets the example of what could be possible. You are demonstrating alignment/ownership of decisions. Others may catch on over time.

    - You are doing your part in making the decisions/ directions work. Again, you are demonstrating alignment in how you are taking on making the decision work.

    - You are visibly supporting the leader/decision-maker. You are being a team player and going beyond your own ego or own agenda to support the leader. Caution: Don't do this in order to look good. It will backfire on you. Do this because you want to support the team in moving toward being an aligned team.

2. Have your voice be heard prior to the time the decision is reached (if, in fact, you are present at a forum
   for doing this). Say what needs to be said. Be straight
   and be open and be thorough. Be willing to stay at
   it until you know you have been heard and there is
   nothing more to say. As I've said before, don't make
   a pest of yourself, so be discerning about this. I don't
   mean don't be afraid – it is fine to be afraid but don't
   let it stop you. If you are going to stop, stop because
   you have discerned that you have said enough and
   that by continuing you will have gone too far.

   • You are demonstrating that straight talk is pos-
     sible; not only possible, but to be desired and
     maybe emulated.

   • You are adding to the conversation your own per-
     spective and your own experience. You are con-
     tributing what you have to contribute.

   • You may be influencing the conversations that
     will have them lead to different conclusions and
     different decisions than would have resulted in
     the conversation if you didn't say what you had
     to say about it.

   • You are establishing a relationship with you team
     members in which they will begin to know that

they can count on you to be straight and be thorough.

3. Ask questions when you don't understand something. Act as if your understanding is critical to the quality of the decision being sought after (it is).

- You are demonstrating a willingness to risk seeming slow or stupid in order to understand something, the understanding of which is critical to the decision-making process.

- You are helping to clarify the issues, thus potentially leading to better decisions. I have rarely found when I ask what could be a stupid question that I was the only one who had that question.

- Along with at least number 2 above, you are establishing yourself as someone who will take a risk when the only thing at stake is what people may think of you or how you will look. If others begin to do this – and even if nothing else that you are doing on this list made a difference – this alone would make an enormous difference in your team's performance and your team dynamics.

4. Request a summary of a decision that is made and either ask that it be recorded or write it down yourself and offer to send it out to the rest of the team. If in a subsequent meeting the same discussion gets going about the same topic, gently remind the team that this issue has already been discussed, that a decision has been reached, and remind them what the decision was. Then, ask if they really want to revisit it. Decisions reached can be revisited when there is new information that might affect that decision, but it is a waste of time if this is not the case.

   • You are helping the team take note of its decisions and potentially saving lots of time and energy. You are also helping to move the meeting along, and to take the meeting seriously enough that you don't want to waste team member's time.

   • You are demonstrating how to do this. These more process-oriented aspects are easier for others to pick up and start doing themselves.

5. Refrain from second-guessing. The term, second-guessing, I have found, has meaning in the U.S. but not necessarily in other countries. It means wanting to have a decision be re-thought after the decision is made; or thinking you know better, especially when

you weren't privy to the decision-making process. If a decision is made and you are not present when the discussion (if there was one) occurred, then it is perfectly okay to ask the decision-maker in an aside: "I am willing to align with this decision, but it would be useful to know what your thinking was that had you make it. Would you mind telling me briefly?" And then if he or she does tell you, then you can just say, "Thank you – I got it." This allows you to practice aligning when you had little or no input to the decision. It keeps you aligned and in the game.

- It may not impact others, but it could have a positive effect on the decision-maker. She or he at some point will understand that you are committed to something you call alignment, and this could trigger a fantastic conversation with an even more fantastic outcome.

- This allows you to practice aligning when you had little or no input to the decision. It keeps you aligned and in the game.

- You are contributing your ability to embrace and to own decisions reached when you were not present to the process. This is a huge issue on many executive teams and others. It can be the cause of serious issues that destroy a team's ability to be a strong team, and sometimes causes deep-set trust issues. Your actions may be a drop in the bucket, but enough drops in a bucket fills it.

6. Ask for feedback. If you are nervous about something you said in a meeting, ask someone who was in the meeting to give you feedback. Tell them you are nervous about the action and you wanted to get their straight response to your request for feedback. As always with feedback, it is a gift given and it is fine to ask questions for clarity, but basically the only response back to them is "Thank you". Especially, do not defend or explain yourself.

- You stop your own mind from beating you up about something you did. It will typically end up with you being encouraged about your participation and embolden you further. If you get negative feedback, then you can correct course the next time. At least you do not have to be fearful of getting any negative feedback, because this has already happened.

- You demonstrate to at least the people you ask that you want their feedback and their straight talk. You are on their side and you are putting them on your side – it is a kind of partnership that can go a long way on a team.

In summary, these are all actions you can take that have nothing to do with anyone but you and your willingness to do them, and they will likely have a positive impact on the team. Each one could have that impact; and taken together you will be transforming how you are viewed as a team member.

One note of caution: Do not be righteous about what a great team player you are. You will turn people off and even against you and you will destroy your own intent in doing all of these things. This entire list of what to do is an exercise in humility, in transcending your ego for the betterment of the team. If you are not getting beyond your ego – if you are doing it for your own self-aggrandizement – you will get what you are asking for and you may not like it; that is, you will get attention to yourself and it may not be the kind of attention you want. These are best seen as servant-leadership acts – you are doing it to serve the team.

WHAT TO DO IN DEALING WITH OTHERS

The last section had to do what you can do, dealing with yourself mostly. It was about your leading by example and thus indirectly influencing others, at least potentially. This section is more about how can you deal with others more directly in a way that influences them toward becoming more effective teammates on a team that is either yet to be aligned or already aligned but still learning.

To do this – to influence others' behaviors by dealing with them directly – is slippery terrain. If you are not cautious, not skillful, then you may do more damage than good. The last thing in the world you would want to become is the person who is always beating a drum that no one else is interested in. You need to be careful that you are not being an overt and obvious evangelist for an aligned team. You will only deepen whatever dysfunctions or difficulties or non-aligned behavior that already exists.

That being said, there are things you can do in addition to being an example and demonstrating effective team behaviors. Here is a list:

1. Certainly if anyone asks you about any of your actions related to your setting an example (from the last section), then that is an open invitation to talk about what you are doing. If for example, someone comes

to you after a meeting and says, "That was very brave of you to tell John that you believed the best action to take would be to wait before we buy that company. You knew he was determined to have it go his way, but you spoke out against it."

You could respond by saying "thank you" and by telling him that you were working on always saying what needs to be said in these meetings. You might add that there really was not anything to be afraid of, that John does not really do anything detrimental to people who disagreed with him (if that is true, of course). You might get into a meaningful dialogue with him. And you might end up encouraging him to do the same.

2. If you are not the leader of the team, and you observe the leader shutting other people down, not listening to them or respecting them, you may be able to talk to her or him on the side and suggest to her that getting open conversation in the room is really important to the quality of the discussions and the possibilities that may emerge. Needless to say, you cannot do this with everybody and not everybody can do this, but if you think you can, give it a try. Be tactful, and don't overdo it.

3. See if you can draw people out during a discussion in a meeting, especially if you think this person would have something to say that would be valuable for the discussion. You might say, for example, "Mary, you've been quiet, and you are the expert on the market in the U.S. I'd like to hear what you have to say about this." Later, you might pull Mary aside and ask her if it was okay that you did that, and that you only wanted to get her to add her experience to the mix. Generally, people are okay with one's having done that, as long as it is not overdone. If she did have a problem with it, consider it a gift that she would say that to you, and hear her out and work it out with her. This is the kind of dialogue that is needed on any team.

4. Whenever you hear anybody complaining about a meeting, or about those meetings in general, or about the team leader or anyone else on the team relative to their team behavior, ask them if they would be willing to talk to the appropriate person about it. If they are willing, ask them when they are going to do it. If they are not willing, ask them why, not in an accusatory manner but just to find out why they would not be willing. You will learn something about the perceived consequences of being straight and open on the team. Sometimes, when you hear a perceived con-

sequence, ask if they really believed that to be true. Usually, when they think about it, people on a team will realize that the perceived consequence is not a likely reality anyway.

I have listed some of the things that you can do directly with others. There are many possibilities. Always be discerning about what you say and to whom. Over time, if you are successful at setting the example and speaking directly to others on the team, you will find that you get more and more leeway and more and more permission to give input and to intervene. Remember, this is a slow process, and every inch of progress takes you closer to your goal.

THIS IS A JOURNEY

Taking on being personally responsible for your team's effectiveness and success is a long journey, and like every other long journey you will run into obstacles and delays and difficulties you could not foresee. If you stay the course and get more and more skillful at doing this, you will begin to see changes occurring around you. You will begin to see others aligning. You will begin to see people speaking up more and being more willing to be in the fray.

What are your options? To just shut up and not take this on and not be responsible for your team's success? That is an option, although not a very satisfying one.

I am reminded of a quote attributed to Michaelangelo:

"The greater danger for most of us is not that our aim is too high and we miss it, but that it is too low and we reach it."

And,

"Risk! Risk anything! Care no more for the opinions of others, for those voices. Do the hardest thing on earth for you. Act for yourself. Face the truth."
—**Katherine Masfield,** *New Zealand short story author* *(1888 - 1923)*

One last piece of advice. I call this a journey because it happens over time. You have to be willing to be in it for the long haul, and one way to do that is to appreciate the small wins and rewards as you go along. Small wins on many teams have big impact. When you get discouraged, do not let it stop you. To take any journey, it is the ability to be unstoppable that predicts one's success or failure. Build a network of people around you that are supportive of what you are doing. They will help you when quitting looks better than staying the course.

CONCLUSION

ALIGNING OTHER TEAMS

IN THE ORGANIZATION

The sense of danger must not disappear:
The way is both short and steep,
However gradual it looks from here;
Look if you like, but you will have to leap.
—**W. H. Auden,** *poet*

It is definitely possible to have aligned teams other than the senior executive team. This is not only possible, but very advantageous to the success of the team and the company. I have spent a great deal of time working with senior management levels who directly report to members of the executive team. This is a particularly powerful group to work with since they are the likely successors to carry on the future of the company. They are also bright, successful, and the critical operational link for fulfilling any new strategic implementation. They are not typically a team themselves in the organizational structure, and depending upon the circumstances, it may or may not be advisable for them to become a team. If they are a team together or if they are not, it is extraordinarily useful for them to embrace the notion of aligned teams. Either way, they can be an additional driving force in an expanded partnership with the executive team in the fulfillment of the future that is being created.

Aligning teams composed of management level people is a whole different ball game. For one thing, they have different challenges. They need to be able to align their decisions with decisions made by the senior executive team. This requires a very tricky series of conversations. I once worked with a publishing company, and it became evident to the CEO and the rest of the team that the alignment of their direct reports was going to be a critical, almost simultaneous, step. In meeting with this larger group of senior managers, it quickly became obvious that the biggest challenge was going to be to overcome the dominant mindset that the executives were cut off from reality with a history of inept leadership and wrong decisions. It took a lengthy series of discussions for the group to be willing to own a different perspective about the executive team and for them to be able to be aligned.

When I work inside an organization with the executive team, they are always excited about aligning others in the company. But I have to tell the executives not to try and take this to their unit or department teams without assistance. The above example about the publishing house may give you some ideas about why, but the following is a list of some things to consider:

- As in the publishing company example, there are potential attitudes and mindsets at the next levels of management that will be difficult to uncover and to deal with effectively by someone from inside the company.

- One extra challenge that managers have is that they need to be able to align on decisions already made by the executive team, typically without their direct input. Even presenting this notion to them may reek of manipulation and a desire to have them succumb to the will of their bosses. If you consider that the development of the individuals in this group for the long term is critical, then having them thinking they are being asked to succumb to the will of others is extremely detrimental.

- They are a larger group than the executive team, and often the larger the group the more difficult and more complex the challenges of having them agree to be aligned.

- They are generally not a team, so the discussions about being an "aligned team" need altering. This is not an insignificant change in how the possibility of being aligned is presented.

- My own experience has shown me that whereas working with executive teams to have them embrace alignment is a relatively similar process no matter what the circumstances, the aligning of the next levels is not. The level of sophistication and experience in doing this and designing the process is critical.

A FINAL WORD

By now you have an understanding of this way of looking at alignment, the value of being an aligned team, and what it is like to go through the process. It may seem daunting (or the reverse, overly simple), but to paraphrase the quote I used earlier by JFK:

> *We choose to [align our executive team] and do the other things, not because they are easy, but because they are hard. Because that goal will serve to organize and measure the best of our energies and skills. Because that challenge is one that we are willing to accept, one that we are unwilling to postpone and one that we intend to win.*

More to the point, we may have said: *We choose to create an extraordinary future for our company...*

My mission is to (1) help executives and companies to take on the challenge of creating extraordinary futures together, and (2) to enable other consultants and coaches to help executives take on those challenges. Not just to take them on, but to be successful at them and to increase their capability to be successful at the next future they create, and the next one. And it is not because it is easy – it isn't easy. This challenge is not only the loftiest one can take in leading an organization, but it is also the one that if you are not taking, then you are not doing the most you can do to ensure the long-term success of that organization.

Executive team alignment creates the foundation for that success. The foundation allows for the possibility of the fulfillment of what has already begun.

Welcome to the journey! Bon voyage!

Miles Kierson

ABOUT THE AUTHOR

Miles Kierson

Mr. Kierson has twenty-five years of professional consulting experience. He is the creator of the ExecuTAP™ world-class executive team alignment process; The Discipline of Execution™ which creates a culture of execution; and The Leadership Journey™ an unparalleled leadership development program. These programs have produced dramatic, sustainable impact on client organizations. President of KiersonConsulting LLC, Miles has trained consultants and coaches from all over the world in facilitating ExecuTAP™.

President of KiersonConsulting LLC, Miles has specialized in executive team alignment and the requirements for fulfillment that flow from that process, especially leadership development associated with strategic implementation, and mobilizing the organization. Miles is a former vice president of CSC Strategic Consulting Services, the re-engineering and leadership development consulting arm of CSC. Over the span of his career, Miles' clients have ranged from small companies to Fortune 200 companies in many industries including oil, electric utilities, retail, financial services, telecommunications, and manufacturing. He has a Master's Degree in Spiritual Psychology, and has completed coursework with many leading traditional and non-traditional thinkers. He was also a Senior Vice President at a large commercial real estate brokerage.

Register on our website for a free gift and receive more information and updates

www.kiersonconsulting.com

CPSIA information can be obtained at www.ICGtesting.com
Printed in the USA
LVOW051530240213

321472LV00002B/5/P